EXPLORATIONS

APOLLO 11

BY DALTON RAINS

WWW.APEXEDITIONS.COM

Copyright © 2025 by Apex Editions, Mendota Heights, MN 55120. All rights reserved. No part of this book may be reproduced or utilized in any form or by any means without written permission from the publisher.

Apex is distributed by North Star Editions:
sales@northstareditions.com | 888-417-0195

Produced for Apex by Red Line Editorial.

Photographs ©: Neil A. Armstrong/NASA, cover; NASA, 1, 4–5, 10–11, 16–17, 18, 19, 20–21, 22–23, 24–25, 26, 27, 29; Shutterstock Images, 6–7, 8–9, 13, 14–15

Library of Congress Control Number: 2024939710

ISBN
979-8-89250-325-9 (hardcover)
979-8-89250-363-1 (paperback)
979-8-89250-436-2 (ebook pdf)
979-8-89250-401-0 (hosted ebook)

Printed in the United States of America
Mankato, MN
012025

NOTE TO PARENTS AND EDUCATORS
Apex books are designed to build literacy skills in striving readers. Exciting, high-interest content attracts and holds readers' attention. The text is carefully leveled to allow students to achieve success quickly. Additional features, such as bolded glossary words for difficult terms, help build comprehension.

CHAPTER 1
LIFTOFF! 4

CHAPTER 2
TO THE MOON 10

CHAPTER 3
TOUCHING DOWN 16

CHAPTER 4
BIG IMPACT 22

COMPREHENSION QUESTIONS • 28
GLOSSARY • 30
TO LEARN MORE • 31
ABOUT THE AUTHOR • 31
INDEX • 32

CHAPTER 1

LIFTOFF!

On July 16, 1969, three **astronauts** boarded a huge rocket. A small spacecraft sat at the top. It would try to reach the moon.

The Saturn V rocket sent astronauts to the moon. This rocket was as tall as a 36-story building.

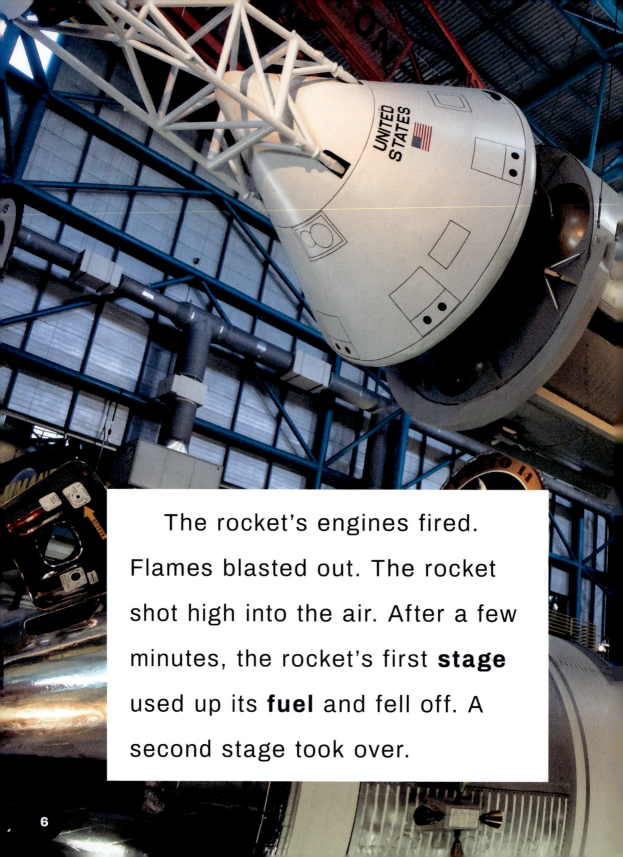

The rocket's engines fired. Flames blasted out. The rocket shot high into the air. After a few minutes, the rocket's first **stage** used up its **fuel** and fell off. A second stage took over.

FAST FACT
The rocket launched from Kennedy Space Center in Florida.

Today, people can visit Kennedy Space Center to see models of the rocket.

By now, the spacecraft was miles above the ground. A third stage sent it even higher. The spacecraft began **orbiting** Earth.

Workers in a control station on the ground helped launch and guide the rocket.

MOON MISSIONS

The launch was part of NASA's Apollo program. The program's goal was to land people on the moon. A series of **missions** tested different steps. Apollo 11 was the first mission that tried to land.

CHAPTER 2

TO THE MOON

The astronauts orbited Earth a few times. Then the rocket's third stage fired its engines again. It pushed the spacecraft toward the moon.

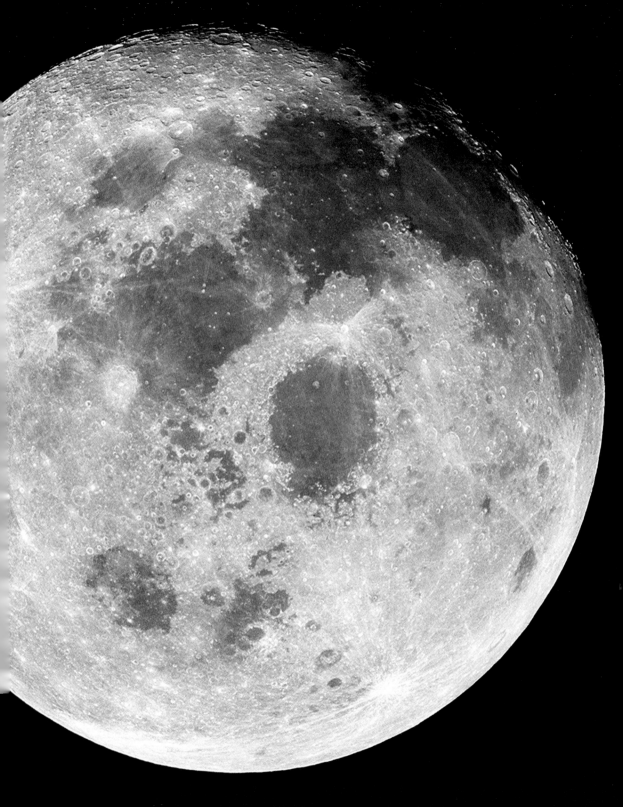

The moon is about 239,000 miles (384,600 km) from Earth.

The journey took three days. Along the way, the spacecraft changed shape. The command **module** and service module moved. They flipped around. Then they **docked** with the lunar module.

THREE PARTS

The Apollo 11 spacecraft had three parts. The crew rode in a command module. That part connected to a service module. A lunar module was for landing on the moon.

The service module provided fuel and power. It attached to the back of the command module.

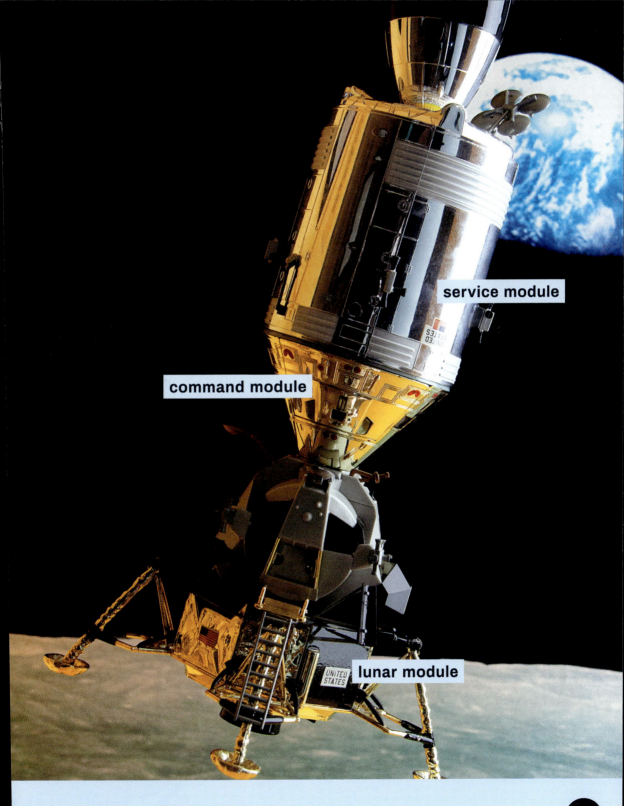

FAST FACT
On July 18, the crew inspected the lunar module. They checked that everything was working.

On July 19, the spacecraft began orbiting the moon. Next, the astronauts got ready to land.

The command module was about the size of a car. Controls and displays covered its walls.

15

CHAPTER 3

TOUCHING DOWN

On July 20, Neil Armstrong and Buzz Aldrin boarded the lunar module. They flew down to the moon's surface. Michael Collins stayed behind.

A small tunnel connected the lunar module to the command module. The astronauts practiced using it.

Armstrong steered the module to a flat area. After landing, he and Aldrin put on spacesuits. They waited for the module to **depressurize**.

A computer controlled most of the landing. But Armstrong trained to steer the lunar module, too.

Each astronaut had different jobs during the mission. Collins (center) took pictures of the moon from orbit. Armstrong (left) and Aldrin explored the moon's surface.

FAST FACT

The astronauts landed in an area called the Sea of Tranquility.

Finally, Armstrong climbed out of the lunar module. He became the first person to step on the moon. Aldrin joined him about 20 minutes later.

A camera on the lunar module took video of Armstrong. Then Armstrong took photos of Aldrin (pictured).

ON TV

The moon landing was broadcast live on TV. More than 600 million people around the world watched. It was one of the most-viewed events of all time.

21

CHAPTER 4

BIG IMPACT

Armstrong and Aldrin gathered **samples**. They took rocks and soil. They also set up tools. The tools sent measurements to Earth.

The astronauts collected more than 45 pounds (20 kg) of material from the moon.

The men stayed outside for more than two hours. Then they returned to the lunar module. They flew up to the command module. From there, the whole crew headed back to Earth.

PACKING LIGHT

To take off, the lunar module needed to be as light as possible. So, the men left some things behind on the moon. They left waste and tools.

The lunar module was on the moon's surface for close to 22 hours.

The command module landed in the Pacific Ocean. A boat brought the astronauts to shore.

The astronauts reached Earth on July 24. The mission was a success. Scientists studied the samples the astronauts brought back. They learned about the moon's history.

FAST FACT
After Apollo 11, five more Apollo missions landed on the moon.

Rock and soil samples helped scientists learn when and how the moon formed.

COMPREHENSION QUESTIONS

Write your answers on a separate piece of paper.

1. Write a few sentences describing the main ideas of Chapter 2.

2. Would you like to travel to the moon? Why or why not?

3. Which astronaut didn't go down to the moon's surface?

  A. Neil Armstrong
  B. Michael Collins
  C. Buzz Aldrin

4. How many total days did the Apollo 11 mission last?

  A. 8
  B. 12
  C. 20

5. What does **inspected** mean in this book?

*On July 18, the crew **inspected** the lunar module. They checked that everything was working.*

- **A.** broke apart
- **B.** stayed away from
- **C.** looked at closely

6. What does **broadcast** mean in this book?

*The moon landing was **broadcast** live on TV. More than 600 million people around the world watched.*

- **A.** shown
- **B.** skipped
- **C.** hurt

Answer key on page 32.

GLOSSARY

astronauts

People who are trained to travel in a spacecraft.

depressurize

To change the air pressure in a space to a lower amount.

docked

Joined together while in space.

fuel

Something that can make power when it is burned.

missions

Plans to send people or objects to space. Each mission often has its own goal.

module

One part of a spacecraft. It connects to other parts.

orbiting

Following a curved path around an object in space.

samples

Small amounts of a material that scientists collect and study.

stage

A part of a rocket that gives it power.

BOOKS

Morey, Allan. *Exploring Space.* Minneapolis: Bellwether Media, 2023.

Murray, Julie. *Famous Space Missions.* Minneapolis: Abdo Publishing, 2022.

Rains, Dalton. *Moon Landings.* Mendota Heights, MN: Apex Editions, 2024.

ONLINE RESOURCES

Visit **www.apexeditions.com** to find links and resources related to this title.

ABOUT THE AUTHOR

Dalton Rains is an author and editor from Saint Paul, Minnesota.

INDEX

A
Aldrin, Buzz, 16, 18, 20, 22
Apollo program, 9, 27
Armstrong, Neil, 16, 18, 20, 22
astronauts, 4, 10, 14, 19, 26

C
Collins, Michael, 16

F
fuel, 6

K
Kennedy Space Center, 7

L
landing, 9, 12, 14, 18–19, 21, 27

M
missions, 9, 26–27
module, 12, 14, 16, 18, 20, 24

O
orbiting, 8, 10, 14

R
rocket, 4, 6–7, 10

S
samples, 22, 26
Sea of Tranquility, 19
spacecraft, 4, 8, 10, 12, 14
stage, 6, 8, 10

ANSWER KEY:
1. Answers will vary; 2. Answers will vary; 3. B; 4. A; 5. C; 6. A